GREATER GRATITUDE

Looking to God to See the Good

This journal is for the one who struggles to see the good, who feels as if they have nothing to be grateful for, and for the one mad at God for their circumstances and feelings they are experiencing. One day, you will step outside to see the sun shining in a big, blue sky as you feel a cool breeze on your face. You will realize that today could've been rainy or cloudy, and instead of feeling mad or gloomy, you will be filled with gratitude.

Through this journal, I pray that you will develop a state of gratitude for who God is and all He has done. While we may not be able to see the good around us, we can always look to God to see the good.

With love, Emily

THIS JOURNAL BELONGS TO:

_____

Date: _____

How would you rate your day?

☆☆☆☆☆

Explain your rating:

_____

_____

_____

Despite your rating, in what ways did you see God today?

_____

_____

_____

How does that relate to God's character?

ie. It shows me that God does care for me.

_____

_____

_____

What are you grateful for today?

ie. I am grateful for a God who cares.

_____

_____

_____

Prayer

ie. Father, thank you for being a God who cares. Help me continue to

see you and Your goodness each and every day.

_____

In Your name I pray, amen.

_____

Action Step: *Spend today memorizing 1 Thessalonians 5:18.*

Date: _____

How would you rate your day?

☆☆☆☆☆

Explain your rating:

_____

_____

_____

Despite your rating, in what ways did you see God today?

_____

_____

_____

How does that relate to God's character?

_____

_____

_____

What are you grateful for today?

_____

_____

_____

Prayer

_____

_____

_____

Action Step: *Call a friend to remind them of why you're grateful for them.*

Date: _____

How would you rate your day?

☆☆☆☆☆

Explain your rating:

_____

_____

_____

Despite your rating, in what ways did you see God today?

_____

_____

_____

How does that relate to God's character?

_____

_____

_____

What are you grateful for today?

_____

_____

_____

Prayer

_____

_____

_____

Action Step: _Give a gift to someone you are grateful for (can be big or small)._

Date: _____

How would you rate your day?

☆☆☆☆☆

Explain your rating:

_____

_____

_____

Despite your rating, in what ways did you see God today?

_____

_____

_____

How does that relate to God's character?

_____

_____

_____

What are you grateful for today?

_____

_____

_____

Prayer

_____

_____

_____

Action Step: _Offer to help a friend in need (grab groceries, mow a lawn, etc.)_

Date: _____

How would you rate your day?

☆ ☆ ☆ ☆ ☆

Explain your rating:

_____

_____

_____

Despite your rating, in what ways did you see God today?

_____

_____

_____

How does that relate to God's character?

_____

_____

_____

What are you grateful for today?

_____

_____

_____

Prayer

_____

_____

_____

Action Step: *Spend five minutes outside to enjoy the weather.*

Date: _____

How would you rate your day?

☆☆☆☆☆

Explain your rating:

_____

_____

_____

Despite your rating, in what ways did you see God today?

_____

_____

_____

How does that relate to God's character?

_____

_____

_____

What are you grateful for today?

_____

_____

_____

Prayer

_____

_____

_____

Action Step: *Write a letter to someone expressing your gratitude.*

Date: _____

How would you rate your day?

☆☆☆☆☆

Explain your rating:

_____

_____

_____

Despite your rating, in what ways did
you see God today?

_____

_____

_____

How does that relate to God's character?

_____

_____

_____

What are you grateful for today?

_____

_____

_____

Prayer

_____

_____

_____

Action Step: _Take a 10 minute walk and take note of the things that you are grateful for._

Date: _____

How would you rate your day?

☆☆☆☆☆

Explain your rating:

_____

_____

_____

Despite your rating, in what ways did you see God today?

_____

_____

_____

How does that relate to God's character?

_____

_____

_____

What are you grateful for today?

_____

_____

_____

Prayer

_____

_____

_____

Action Step: *Bake cookies for someone you're grateful for.*

Date: _____

How would you rate your day?

☆☆☆☆☆

Explain your rating:

_____

_____

_____

Despite your rating, in what ways did
you see God today?

_____

_____

_____

How does that relate to God's character?

_____

_____

_____

What are you grateful for today?

_____

_____

_____

Prayer

_____

_____

_____

Action Step: _Invite a friend over for dinner._

Date: _____

How would you rate your day?

☆☆☆☆☆

Explain your rating:

_____

_____

_____

Despite your rating, in what ways did
you see God today?

_____

_____

_____

How does that relate to God's character?

_____

_____

_____

What are you grateful for today?

_____

_____

_____

Prayer

_____

_____

_____

Action Step: *Have a conversation with a friend and give them your full attention.*

"Gratitude isn't only a celebration when good things happen; Gratitude is a declaration that God is good no matter what happens."
Ann Voskamp

Date: _____

How would you rate your day?

☆☆☆☆☆

Explain your rating:

_____

_____

_____

Despite your rating, in what ways did you see God today?

_____

_____

_____

How does that relate to God's character?

_____

_____

_____

What are you grateful for today?

_____

_____

_____

Prayer

_____

_____

_____

Action Step: *Spend today memorizing Psalm 95:2.*

Date: _____

How would you rate your day?

☆☆☆☆☆

Explain your rating:

_____

_____

_____

Despite your rating, in what ways did you see God today?

_____

_____

_____

How does that relate to God's character?

_____

_____

_____

What are you grateful for today?

_____

_____

_____

Prayer

_____

_____

_____

Action Step: *Print a picture of something/someone you're grateful for and place it where you will see it.*

Date: _____

How would you rate your day?

☆ ☆ ☆ ☆ ☆

Explain your rating:

_____

_____

_____

Despite your rating, in what ways did you see God today?

_____

_____

_____

How does that relate to God's character?

_____

_____

_____

What are you grateful for today?

_____

_____

_____

Prayer

_____

_____

_____

Action Step: _Try something new!_

Date: _____

How would you rate your day?

☆☆☆☆☆

Explain your rating:

_____

_____

_____

Despite your rating, in what ways did you see God today?

_____

_____

_____

How does that relate to God's character?

_____

_____

_____

What are you grateful for today?

_____

_____

_____

Prayer

_____

_____

_____

Action Step: _Give a compliment to someone you're grateful for._

Date: _____

How would you rate your day?

☆☆☆☆☆

Explain your rating:

_____
_____
_____

Despite your rating, in what ways did
you see God today?

_____
_____
_____

How does that relate to God's character?

_____

_____

_____

What are you grateful for today?

_____

_____

_____

Prayer

_____

_____

_____

Action Step: _Give a larger tip than normal._

Date: _____

How would you rate your day?

☆☆☆☆☆

Explain your rating:

_____

_____

_____

Despite your rating, in what ways did
you see God today?

_____

_____

_____

How does that relate to God's character?

_____

_____

_____

What are you grateful for today?

_____

_____

_____

Prayer

_____

_____

_____

Action Step: *Give someone you're grateful for a hug or handshake.*

Date: _____

How would you rate your day?

☆☆☆☆☆

Explain your rating:

_____

_____

_____

Despite your rating, in what ways did you see God today?

_____

_____

_____

How does that relate to God's character?

_____

_____

_____

What are you grateful for today?

_____

_____

_____

Prayer

_____

_____

_____

Action Step: *Invite a coworker to coffee this week.*

Date: _____

How would you rate your day?

☆☆☆☆☆

Explain your rating:

_____

_____

_____

Despite your rating, in what ways did you see God today?

_____

_____

_____

How does that relate to God's character?

_____

_____

_____

What are you grateful for today?

_____

_____

_____

Prayer

_____

_____

_____

Action Step: *Smile at someone when ordering or walking by.*

Date: _____

How would you rate your day?

☆ ☆ ☆ ☆ ☆

Explain your rating:

_____

_____

_____

Despite your rating, in what ways did
you see God today?

_____

_____

_____

How does that relate to God's character?

_____

_____

_____

What are you grateful for today?

_____

_____

_____

Prayer

_____

_____

_____

Action Step: _Write a handwritten note to someone you're grateful for._

Date: _____

How would you rate your day?

☆☆☆☆☆

Explain your rating:

_____
_____
_____

Despite your rating, in what ways did you see God today?

_____
_____
_____

How does that relate to God's character?

_____

_____

_____

What are you grateful for today?

_____

_____

_____

Prayer

_____

_____

_____

Action Step: _Spend time doing something you're passionate about._

"Everything we do should be a result of our gratitude for what God has done for us."
Lauryn Hill

Date: _____

How would you rate your day?

☆ ☆ ☆ ☆ ☆

Explain your rating:

_____

_____

_____

Despite your rating, in what ways did you see God today?

_____

_____

_____

How does that relate to God's character?

_____

_____

_____

What are you grateful for today?

_____

_____

_____

Prayer

_____

_____

_____

Action Step: _Spend today memorizing 1 Corinthians 15:57._

Date: _____

How would you rate your day?

☆☆☆☆☆

Explain your rating:

_____

_____

_____

Despite your rating, in what ways did
you see God today?

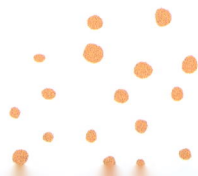

_____

_____

_____

How does that relate to God's character?

_____

_____

_____

What are you grateful for today?

_____

_____

_____

Prayer

_____

_____

_____

Action Step: *Text a friend to remind them that you're grateful for them.*

Date: _____

How would you rate your day?

☆☆☆☆☆

Explain your rating:

_____

_____

_____

Despite your rating, in what ways did you see God today?

_____

_____

_____

How does that relate to God's character?

_____

_____

_____

What are you grateful for today?

_____

_____

_____

Prayer

_____

_____

_____

Action Step: *Surprise someone by paying for their order.*

Date: _____

How would you rate your day?

☆☆☆☆☆

Explain your rating:

_____

_____

_____

Despite your rating, in what ways did you see God today?

_____

_____

_____

How does that relate to God's character?

_____

_____

_____

What are you grateful for today?

_____

_____

_____

Prayer

_____

_____

_____

Action Step: *Catch up with the friend that you gave your full attention to.*

Date: _____

How would you rate your day?

☆☆☆☆☆

Explain your rating:

_____

_____

_____

Despite your rating, in what ways did you see God today?

_____

_____

_____

How does that relate to God's character?

_____

_____

_____

What are you grateful for today?

_____

_____

_____

Prayer

_____

_____

_____

Action Step: _Post a note somewhere that says, "I am grateful for you!"_

Date: _____

How would you rate your day?

☆☆☆☆☆

Explain your rating:

_____

_____

_____

Despite your rating, in what ways did you see God today?

_____

_____

_____

How does that relate to God's character?

_____

_____

_____

What are you grateful for today?

_____

_____

_____

Prayer

_____

_____

_____

Action Step: *Donate something to a friend in need.*

Date: _____

How would you rate your day?

☆ ☆ ☆ ☆ ☆

Explain your rating:

_____

_____

_____

Despite your rating, in what ways did you see God today?

_____

_____

_____

How does that relate to God's character?

_____

_____

_____

What are you grateful for today?

_____

_____

_____

Prayer

_____

_____

_____

Action Step: *Check in on someone and see how they are doing.*

Date: _____

How would you rate your day?

☆☆☆☆☆

Explain your rating:

_____

_____

_____

Despite your rating, in what ways did you see God today?

_____

_____

_____

How does that relate to God's character?

_____

_____

_____

What are you grateful for today?

_____

_____

_____

Prayer

_____

_____

_____

Action Step: _Ask for cash back and gift it to the cashier._

Date: _____

How would you rate your day?

☆☆☆☆☆

Explain your rating:

_____

_____

_____

Despite your rating, in what ways did
you see God today?

_____

_____

_____

How does that relate to God's character?

_____

_____

_____

What are you grateful for today?

_____

_____

_____

Prayer

_____

_____

_____

Action Step: _Offer to pick up someone's lunch or coffee order._

Date: _____

How would you rate your day?

☆☆☆☆☆

Explain your rating:

_____

_____

_____

Despite your rating, in what ways did you see God today?

_____

_____

_____

How does that relate to God's character?

_____

_____

_____

What are you grateful for today?

_____

_____

_____

Prayer

_____

_____

_____

Action Step: *Say "thank you" to someone you're grateful for.*

"To be grateful is to recognize the love of God in everything He has given - and He has given us everything."
Thomas Merton

Date: _____

How would you rate your day?

☆☆☆☆☆

Explain your rating:

_____

_____

_____

Despite your rating, in what ways did you see God today?

_____

_____

_____

How does that relate to God's character?

_____

_____

_____

What are you grateful for today?

_____

_____

_____

Prayer

_____

_____

_____

Action Step: *Spend today memorizing 1 Chronicles 16:34.*

Date: _____

How would you rate your day?

☆☆☆☆☆

Explain your rating:

_____

_____

_____

Despite your rating, in what ways did you see God today?

_____

_____

_____

How does that relate to God's character?

_____

_____

_____

What are you grateful for today?

_____

_____

_____

Prayer

_____

_____

_____

Action Step: _Call a friend to remind them of why you're grateful for them._

Date: _____

How would you rate your day?

☆☆☆☆☆

Explain your rating:

_____

_____

_____

Despite your rating, in what ways did
you see God today?

_____

_____

_____

How does that relate to God's character?

_____

_____

_____

What are you grateful for today?

_____

_____

_____

Prayer

_____

_____

_____

Action Step: _Give a gift to someone you are grateful for (can be big or small)._

Date: _____

How would you rate your day?

☆☆☆☆☆

Explain your rating:

_____

_____

_____

Despite your rating, in what ways did you see God today?

_____

_____

_____

How does that relate to God's character?

_____

_____

_____

What are you grateful for today?

_____

_____

_____

Prayer

_____

_____

_____

Action Step: _Offer to help a friend in need (grab groceries, mow a lawn, etc.)_

Date: _____

How would you rate your day?

☆☆☆☆☆

Explain your rating:

_____

_____

_____

Despite your rating, in what ways did
you see God today?

_____

_____

_____

How does that relate to God's character?

_____

_____

_____

What are you grateful for today?

_____

_____

_____

Prayer

_____

_____

_____

Action Step: _Spend five minutes outside to enjoy the weather._

Date: _____

How would you rate your day?

☆☆☆☆☆

Explain your rating:

_____

_____

_____

Despite your rating, in what ways did you see God today?

_____

_____

_____

How does that relate to God's character?

_____

_____

_____

What are you grateful for today?

_____

_____

_____

Prayer

_____

_____

_____

Action Step: _Write a letter to someone expressing your gratitude._

Date: _____

How would you rate your day?

☆ ☆ ☆ ☆ ☆

Explain your rating:

_____

_____

_____

Despite your rating, in what ways did you see God today?

_____

_____

_____

How does that relate to God's character?

_____

_____

_____

What are you grateful for today?

_____

_____

_____

Prayer

_____

_____

_____

Action Step: *Take a 10 minute walk and take note of the things that you are grateful for.*

Date: _____

How would you rate your day?

☆ ☆ ☆ ☆ ☆

Explain your rating:

_____

_____

_____

Despite your rating, in what ways did
you see God today?

_____

_____

_____

How does that relate to God's character?

_____

_____

_____

What are you grateful for today?

_____

_____

_____

Prayer

_____

_____

_____

Action Step: *Bake cookies for someone you're grateful for.*

Date: _____

How would you rate your day?

☆☆☆☆☆

Explain your rating:

_____

_____

_____

Despite your rating, in what ways did you see God today?

_____

_____

_____

How does that relate to God's character?

_____

_____

_____

What are you grateful for today?

_____

_____

_____

Prayer

_____

_____

_____

Action Step: *Invite a friend over for dinner.*

Date: _____

How would you rate your day?

☆☆☆☆☆

Explain your rating:

_____

_____

_____

Despite your rating, in what ways did you see God today?

_____

_____

_____

How does that relate to God's character?

_____

_____

_____

What are you grateful for today?

_____

_____

_____

Prayer

_____

_____

_____

Action Step: *Have a conversation with a friend and give them your full attention.*

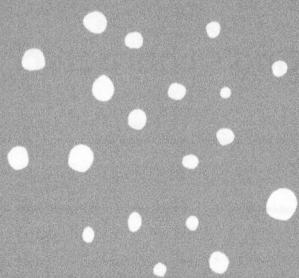

"Giving thanks IN everything shows a heart of faith that God is bigger than the difficulties and that He can use them, if you approach Him with the right heart and spirit, for your good and His glory."
Tony Evans

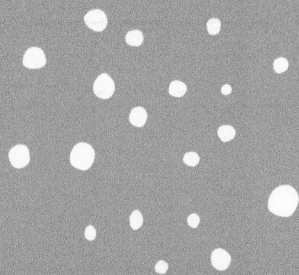

How would you rate your day?

☆☆☆☆☆

Explain your rating:

_____

_____

_____

Despite your rating, in what ways did you see God today?

_____

_____

_____

How does that relate to God's character?

_____

_____

_____

What are you grateful for today?

_____

_____

_____

Prayer

_____

_____

_____

Action Step: *Spend today memorizing 1 Timothy 4:4-5.*

Date: _____

How would you rate your day?

☆ ☆ ☆ ☆ ☆

Explain your rating:

_____

_____

_____

Despite your rating, in what ways did you see God today?

_____

_____

_____

How does that relate to God's character?

_____

_____

_____

What are you grateful for today?

_____

_____

_____

Prayer

_____

_____

_____

Action Step: *Take a picture of something you're grateful for.*

Date: _____

How would you rate your day?

☆ ☆ ☆ ☆ ☆

Explain your rating:

_____

_____

_____

Despite your rating, in what ways did you see God today?

_____

_____

_____

How does that relate to God's character?

_____

_____

_____

What are you grateful for today?

_____

_____

_____

Prayer

_____

_____

_____

Action Step: *Try something new!*

Date: _____

How would you rate your day?

☆☆☆☆☆

Explain your rating:

_____

_____

_____

Despite your rating, in what ways did you see God today?

_____

_____

_____

How does that relate to God's character?

_____

_____

_____

What are you grateful for today?

_____

_____

_____

Prayer

_____

_____

_____

Action Step: _Give a compliment to someone you're grateful for._

Date: _____

How would you rate your day?

☆☆☆☆☆

Explain your rating:

_____

_____

_____

Despite your rating, in what ways did you see God today?

_____

_____

_____

How does that relate to God's character?

_____

_____

_____

What are you grateful for today?

_____

_____

_____

Prayer

_____

_____

_____

Action Step: *Give a larger tip than normal.*

Date: _____

How would you rate your day?

☆ ☆ ☆ ☆ ☆

Explain your rating:

_____

_____

_____

Despite your rating, in what ways did you see God today?

_____

_____

_____

How does that relate to God's character?

_____

_____

_____

What are you grateful for today?

_____

_____

_____

Prayer

_____

_____

_____

Action Step: _Give a hug or handshake to someone you're grateful for._

Date: _____

How would you rate your day?

☆☆☆☆☆

Explain your rating:

_____
_____
_____

Despite your rating, in what ways did you see God today?

_____
_____
_____

How does that relate to God's character?

_____

_____

_____

What are you grateful for today?

_____

_____

_____

Prayer

_____

_____

_____

Action Step: _Invite a coworker to coffee this week._

Date: _____

How would you rate your day?

☆☆☆☆☆

Explain your rating:

_____

_____

_____

Despite your rating, in what ways did
you see God today?

_____

_____

_____

How does that relate to God's character?

_____

_____

_____

What are you grateful for today?

_____

_____

_____

Prayer

_____

_____

_____

Action Step: _Smile at someone when ordering or walking by._

Date: _____

How would you rate your day?

☆ ☆ ☆ ☆ ☆

Explain your rating:

_____

_____

_____

Despite your rating, in what ways did you see God today?

_____

_____

_____

How does that relate to God's character?

_____

_____

_____

What are you grateful for today?

_____

_____

_____

Prayer

_____

_____

_____

Action Step: *Write a handwritten note to someone you're grateful for.*

Date: _____

How would you rate your day?

☆☆☆☆☆

Explain your rating:

_____
_____
_____

Despite your rating, in what ways did you see God today?

_____
_____
_____

How does that relate to God's character?

_____

_____

_____

What are you grateful for today?

_____

_____

_____

Prayer

_____

_____

_____

Action Step: *Spend time doing something you're passionate about.*

"Gratitude is a decision of the will, and if a decision of the will, the choice resides squarely with us. Deciding to be thankful is no easy task. It takes work."
Chuck Swindoll

Date: _____

How would you rate your day?

☆☆☆☆☆

Explain your rating:

_____

_____

_____

Despite your rating, in what ways did
you see God today?

_____

_____

_____

How does that relate to God's character?

_____

_____

_____

What are you grateful for today?

_____

_____

_____

Prayer

_____

_____

_____

Action Step: *Spend today memorizing 1 Samuel 12:24.*

Date: _____

How would you rate your day?

☆☆☆☆☆

Explain your rating:

_____

_____

_____

Despite your rating, in what ways did you see God today?

_____

_____

_____

How does that relate to God's character?

_____

_____

_____

What are you grateful for today?

_____

_____

_____

Prayer

_____

_____

_____

Action Step: *Text a friend to remind them that you're grateful for them.*

Date: _____

How would you rate your day?

☆☆☆☆☆

Explain your rating:

_____

_____

_____

Despite your rating, in what ways did
you see God today?

_____

_____

_____

How does that relate to God's character?

_____

_____

_____

What are you grateful for today?

_____

_____

_____

Prayer

_____

_____

_____

Action Step: *Surprise someone by paying for their order.*

Date: _____

How would you rate your day?

☆☆☆☆☆

Explain your rating:

_____

_____

_____

Despite your rating, in what ways did
you see God today?

_____

_____

_____

How does that relate to God's character?

_____

_____

_____

What are you grateful for today?

_____

_____

_____

Prayer

_____

_____

_____

Action Step: _Catch up with the friend that you gave your full attention to._

Date: _____

How would you rate your day?

☆☆☆☆☆

Explain your rating:

_____

_____

_____

Despite your rating, in what ways did
you see God today?

_____

_____

_____

How does that relate to God's character?

_____

_____

_____

What are you grateful for today?

_____

_____

_____

Prayer

_____

_____

_____

Action Step: *Post a note somewhere that says, "I am grateful for you!"*

Date: _____

How would you rate your day?

☆☆☆☆☆

Explain your rating:

_____

_____

_____

Despite your rating, in what ways did you see God today?

_____

_____

_____

How does that relate to God's character?

_____

_____

_____

What are you grateful for today?

_____

_____

_____

Prayer

_____

_____

_____

Action Step: *Donate something to a friend in need.*

Date: _____

How would you rate your day?

☆ ☆ ☆ ☆ ☆

Explain your rating:

_____

_____

_____

Despite your rating, in what ways did
you see God today?

_____

_____

_____

How does that relate to God's character?

_____

_____

_____

What are you grateful for today?

_____

_____

_____

Prayer

_____

_____

_____

Action Step: *Check in on someone and see how they are doing.*

Date: _____

How would you rate your day?

☆☆☆☆☆

Explain your rating:

_____

_____

_____

Despite your rating, in what ways did you see God today?

_____

_____

_____

How does that relate to God's character?

_____

_____

_____

What are you grateful for today?

_____

_____

_____

Prayer

_____

_____

_____

Action Step: _Ask for cash back and gift it to the cashier._

Date: _____

How would you rate your day?

☆ ☆ ☆ ☆ ☆

Explain your rating:

_____

_____

_____

Despite your rating, in what ways did
you see God today?

_____

_____

_____

How does that relate to God's character?

_____

_____

_____

What are you grateful for today?

_____

_____

_____

Prayer

_____

_____

_____

Action Step: *Offer to pick up someone's lunch or coffee order.*

Date: _____

How would you rate your day?

☆☆☆☆☆

Explain your rating:

_____

_____

_____

Despite your rating, in what ways did
you see God today?

_____

_____

_____

How does that relate to God's character?

_____

_____

_____

What are you grateful for today?

_____

_____

_____

Prayer

_____

_____

_____

Action Step: _Say "thank you" to someone you're grateful for._

"We ought to give thanks for all fortune: if it is good, because it is good, if bad, because it works in us patience, humility and the contempt of this world and the hope of our eternal country."
C.S. Lewis

Date: _____

How would you rate your day?

☆ ☆ ☆ ☆ ☆

Explain your rating:

_____

_____

_____

Despite your rating, in what ways did
you see God today?

_____

_____

_____

How does that relate to God's character?

_____

_____

_____

What are you grateful for today?

_____

_____

_____

Prayer

_____

_____

_____

Action Step: *Spend today memorizing Romans 8:28.*

Date: _____

How would you rate your day?

☆☆☆☆☆

Explain your rating:

_____

_____

_____

Despite your rating, in what ways did you see God today?

_____

_____

_____

How does that relate to God's character?

_____

_____

_____

What are you grateful for today?

_____

_____

_____

Prayer

_____

_____

_____

Action Step: _Call a friend to remind them of why you're grateful for them._

Date: _____

How would you rate your day?

☆ ☆ ☆ ☆ ☆

Explain your rating:

_____

_____

_____

Despite your rating, in what ways did you see God today?

_____

_____

_____

How does that relate to God's character?

_____

_____

_____

What are you grateful for today?

_____

_____

_____

Prayer

_____

_____

_____

Action Step: *Give a gift to someone you are grateful for (can be big or small).*

Date: _____

How would you rate your day?

☆☆☆☆☆

Explain your rating:

_____

_____

_____

Despite your rating, in what ways did you see God today?

_____

_____

_____

How does that relate to God's character?

_____

_____

_____

What are you grateful for today?

_____

_____

_____

Prayer

_____

_____

_____

Action Step: *Offer to help a friend in need (grab groceries, mow a lawn, etc.)*

Date: _____

How would you rate your day?

☆ ☆ ☆ ☆ ☆

Explain your rating:

_____

_____

_____

Despite your rating, in what ways did
you see God today?

_____

_____

_____

How does that relate to God's character?

_____

_____

_____

What are you grateful for today?

_____

_____

_____

Prayer

_____

_____

_____

Action Step: *Spend five minutes outside to enjoy the weather.*

Date: _____

How would you rate your day?

☆☆☆☆☆

Explain your rating:

_____

_____

_____

Despite your rating, in what ways did you see God today?

_____

_____

_____

How does that relate to God's character?

_____

_____

_____

What are you grateful for today?

_____

_____

_____

Prayer

_____

_____

_____

Action Step: *Write a letter to someone expressing your gratitude.*

Date: _____

How would you rate your day?

☆☆☆☆☆

Explain your rating:

_____

_____

_____

Despite your rating, in what ways did you see God today?

_____

_____

_____

How does that relate to God's character?

_____

_____

_____

What are you grateful for today?

_____

_____

_____

Prayer

_____

_____

_____

Action Step: *Take a 10 minute walk and take note of the things that you are grateful for.*

Date: _____

How would you rate your day?

☆☆☆☆☆

Explain your rating:

_____

_____

_____

Despite your rating, in what ways did you see God today?

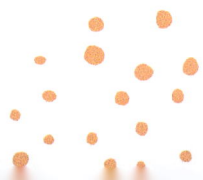

_____

_____

_____

How does that relate to God's character?

_____

_____

_____

What are you grateful for today?

_____

_____

_____

Prayer

_____

_____

_____

Action Step: *Bake cookies for someone you're grateful for.*

Date: _____

How would you rate your day?

☆☆☆☆☆

Explain your rating:

_____

_____

_____

Despite your rating, in what ways did you see God today?

_____

_____

_____

How does that relate to God's character?

_____

_____

_____

What are you grateful for today?

_____

_____

_____

Prayer

_____

_____

_____

Action Step: _Invite a friend over for dinner._

Date: _____

How would you rate your day?

☆☆☆☆☆

Explain your rating:

_____
_____
_____

Despite your rating, in what ways did
you see God today?

_____
_____
_____

How does that relate to God's character?

_____

_____

_____

What are you grateful for today?

_____

_____

_____

Prayer

_____

_____

_____

Action Step: *Have a conversation with a friend and give them your full attention.*

"Gratitude is an offering precious in the sight of God, and it is one that the poorest of us can make and be not poorer but richer for having made it."
A.W. Tozer

Date: _____

How would you rate your day?

☆ ☆ ☆ ☆ ☆

Explain your rating:

_____

_____

_____

Despite your rating, in what ways did you see God today?

_____

_____

_____

How does that relate to God's character?

_____

_____

_____

What are you grateful for today?

_____

_____

_____

Prayer

_____

_____

_____

Action Step: _Spend today memorizing Proverbs 15:30._

Date: _____

How would you rate your day?

☆☆☆☆☆

Explain your rating:

_____

_____

_____

Despite your rating, in what ways did
you see God today?

_____

_____

_____

How does that relate to God's character?

_____

_____

_____

What are you grateful for today?

_____

_____

_____

Prayer

_____

_____

_____

Action Step: *Take a picture of something you're grateful for.*

Date: _____

How would you rate your day?

☆☆☆☆☆

Explain your rating:

_____

_____

_____

Despite your rating, in what ways did
you see God today?

_____

_____

_____

How does that relate to God's character?

_____

_____

_____

What are you grateful for today?

_____

_____

_____

Prayer

_____

_____

_____

Action Step: _Try something new!_

Date: _____

How would you rate your day?

☆☆☆☆☆

Explain your rating:

_____

_____

_____

Despite your rating, in what ways did you see God today?

_____

_____

_____

How does that relate to God's character?

_____

_____

_____

What are you grateful for today?

_____

_____

_____

Prayer

_____

_____

_____

Action Step: *Give a compliment to someone you're grateful for.*

Date: _____

How would you rate your day?

☆☆☆☆☆

Explain your rating:

_____

_____

_____

Despite your rating, in what ways did
you see God today?

_____

_____

_____

How does that relate to God's character?

_____

_____

_____

What are you grateful for today?

_____

_____

_____

Prayer

_____

_____

_____

Action Step: _Give a larger tip than normal._

Date: _____

How would you rate your day?

☆☆☆☆☆

Explain your rating:

_____

_____

_____

Despite your rating, in what ways did you see God today?

_____

_____

_____

How does that relate to God's character?

_____

_____

_____

What are you grateful for today?

_____

_____

_____

Prayer

_____

_____

_____

Action Step: *Give someone you're grateful for a hug or handshake.*

Date: _____

How would you rate your day?

☆☆☆☆☆

Explain your rating:

_____

_____

_____

Despite your rating, in what ways did
you see God today?

_____

_____

_____

How does that relate to God's character?

_____

_____

_____

What are you grateful for today?

_____

_____

_____

Prayer

_____

_____

_____

Action Step: *Invite a coworker to coffee this week.*

Date: _____

How would you rate your day?

☆☆☆☆☆

Explain your rating:

_____
_____
_____

Despite your rating, in what ways did
you see God today?

_____
_____
_____

How does that relate to God's character?

_____

_____

_____

What are you grateful for today?

_____

_____

_____

Prayer

_____

_____

_____

Action Step: *Smile at someone when ordering or walking by.*

Date: _____

How would you rate your day?

☆ ☆ ☆ ☆ ☆

Explain your rating:

_____

_____

_____

Despite your rating, in what ways did you see God today?

_____

_____

_____

How does that relate to God's character?

_____

_____

_____

What are you grateful for today?

_____

_____

_____

Prayer

_____

_____

_____

Action Step: *Write a handwritten note to someone you're grateful for.*

Date: _____

How would you rate your day?

☆☆☆☆☆

Explain your rating:

_____

_____

_____

Despite your rating, in what ways did you see God today?

_____

_____

_____

How does that relate to God's character?

_____

_____

_____

What are you grateful for today?

_____

_____

_____

Prayer

_____

_____

_____

Action Step: *Spend time doing something you're passionate about.*

"Gratitude produces deep, abiding joy because we know that God is working in us, even through difficulties."
Charles Stanley

Date: _____

How would you rate your day?

☆ ☆ ☆ ☆ ☆

Explain your rating:

_____

_____

_____

Despite your rating, in what ways did
you see God today?

_____

_____

_____

How does that relate to God's character?

_____

_____

_____

What are you grateful for today?

_____

_____

_____

Prayer

_____

_____

_____

Action Step: *Spend today memorizing Psalm 118:24.*

Date: _____

How would you rate your day?

☆☆☆☆☆

Explain your rating:

_____

_____

_____

Despite your rating, in what ways did you see God today?

_____

_____

_____

How does that relate to God's character?

_____

_____

_____

What are you grateful for today?

_____

_____

_____

Prayer

_____

_____

_____

Action Step: *Text a friend to remind them that you're grateful for them.*

Date: _____

How would you rate your day?

☆☆☆☆☆

Explain your rating:

_____

_____

_____

Despite your rating, in what ways did
you see God today?

_____

_____

_____

How does that relate to God's character?

_____

_____

_____

What are you grateful for today?

_____

_____

_____

Prayer

_____

_____

_____

Action Step: *Surprise someone by paying for their order.*

Date: _____

How would you rate your day?

☆☆☆☆☆

Explain your rating:

_____

_____

_____

Despite your rating, in what ways did
you see God today?

_____

_____

_____

How does that relate to God's character?

_____

_____

_____

What are you grateful for today?

_____

_____

_____

Prayer

_____

_____

_____

Action Step: _Catch up with the friend that you gave your full attention to._

Date: _____

How would you rate your day?

☆☆☆☆☆

Explain your rating:

_____

_____

_____

Despite your rating, in what ways did you see God today?

_____

_____

_____

How does that relate to God's character?

_____

_____

_____

What are you grateful for today?

_____

_____

_____

Prayer

_____

_____

_____

Action Step: *Post a note somewhere that says, "I am grateful for you!"*

Date: _____

How would you rate your day?

☆☆☆☆☆

Explain your rating:

_____

_____

_____

Despite your rating, in what ways did
you see God today?

_____

_____

_____

How does that relate to God's character?

_____

_____

_____

What are you grateful for today?

_____

_____

_____

Prayer

_____

_____

_____

Action Step: _Donate something to a friend in need._

Date: _____

How would you rate your day?

☆ ☆ ☆ ☆ ☆

Explain your rating:

_____

_____

_____

Despite your rating, in what ways did you see God today?

_____

_____

_____

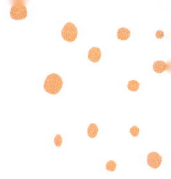

How does that relate to God's character?

_____

_____

_____

What are you grateful for today?

_____

_____

_____

Prayer

_____

_____

_____

Action Step: *Check in on someone and see how they are doing.*

Date: _____

How would you rate your day?

☆☆☆☆☆

Explain your rating:

_____
_____
_____

Despite your rating, in what ways did you see God today?

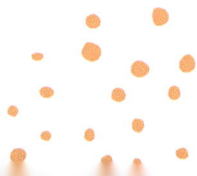

_____
_____
_____

How does that relate to God's character?

_____

_____

_____

What are you grateful for today?

_____

_____

_____

Prayer

_____

_____

_____

Action Step: *Ask for cash back and gift it to the cashier.*

Date: _____

How would you rate your day?

☆☆☆☆☆

Explain your rating:

_____

_____

_____

Despite your rating, in what ways did
you see God today?

_____

_____

_____

How does that relate to God's character?

_____

_____

_____

What are you grateful for today?

_____

_____

_____

Prayer

_____

_____

_____

Action Step: *Offer to pick up someone's lunch or coffee order.*

Date: _____

How would you rate your day?

☆ ☆ ☆ ☆ ☆

Explain your rating:

_____

_____

_____

Despite your rating, in what ways did you see God today?

_____

_____

_____

How does that relate to God's character?

_____

_____

_____

What are you grateful for today?

_____

_____

_____

Prayer

_____

_____

_____

Action Step: *Say "thank you" to someone you're grateful for.*

"God is in control, and therefore in EVERYTHING I can give thanks - not because of the situation but because of the One who directs and rules over it."
Kay Arthur

A YEAR IN PIXELS

	J	F	M	A	M	J	J	A	S	O	N	D
01												
02												
03												
04												
05												
06												
07												
08												
09												
10												
11												
12												
13												
14												
15												
16												
17												
18												
19												
20												
21												
22												
23												
24												
25												
26												
27												
28												
29												
30												
31												

Use a colored pencil or markers to color your mood for each day of the year. Create your own color key below:

COLOR KEY

☐ *ie. Amazing Day!* _____

☐ _____

☐ _____

☐ _____

☐ _____

☐ _____

☐ _____

☐ _____

☐ _____

☐ _____

☐ _____

No matter what our day looks like or how we might feel, learn to look to God in each day and see the good.

References

1.Compiled & Edited by Crosswalk Editorial Staff. "30 Beautiful Thankfulness Quotes to Bring Blessings of Joy and Gratitude." Crosswalk.com, Crosswalk.com, 13 Oct. 2020, https://www.crosswalk.com/faith/spiritual-life/inspiring-quotes/30-christian-quotes-about-thankfulness.html? utm_source=canva&utm_medium=iframely.

2.Hill, Lauryn. "Lauryn Hill Quotes." AZ Quotes, AZ Quotes, https://www.azquotes.com/quote/132469? utm_source=canva&utm_medium=iframely.

3. "Quotes To Note." Paul Madson, Paul Madson, 25 June 2015, https://paulmadson.com/2015/06/25/quotes-to-note/? utm_source=canva&utm_medium=iframely.

Milton Keynes UK
Ingram Content Group UK Ltd.
UKHW020118241124
451423UK00010B/853

9 781088 094143